www.booksbyboxer.com

No part of this publication may be reproduced or
transmitted in any form or by any means, electronic or
mechanical, including photocopying, recording or any
information storage and retrieval system, or for the source
of ideas without written permission from the publisher.

Bee Three Publishing is an imprint of Books By Boxer
Published by
Books By Boxer, Leeds, LS13 4BS UK
Books by Boxer (EU), Dublin, D02 P593, IRELAND
Boxer Gifts LLC, 955 Sawtooth Oak Cir, VA 22802, USA
© Books By Boxer 2024
All Rights Reserved
MADE IN CHINA
ISBN: 9781915410764

This book is produced from responsibly sourced paper
to ensure forest management

"SAAN KONE MYAY LAY"

ဆန်ကုန်မြေလေ

(SAHN-CONE-ME-YAY-LAY)

LANGUAGE: BURMESE

ORIGIN: MYANMAR

MEANING:

THIS PHRASE IS MORE OF A GENERAL INSULT, CALLING
SOMEONE A 'RICE WASTING, EARTH-BURDENING THING'- AND
WHO WANTS TO BE KNOWN AS SOMEONE WHO WASTES RICE?!

"BELLEND"

(BEH-LEND)

LANGUAGE: ENGLISH

ORIGIN: ENGLAND

MEANING:

NAMED AFTER THE GLANS OF THE PENIS, BELLEND IS NOW USE IN THE BRITISH ISLES AS ANOTHER WORD FOR 'DICKHEAD' OR 'TWAT' - THE GENITALS ARE A COMMON THEME!

"PUTAIN"

(POO-TAN)

LANGUAGE: FRENCH

ORIGIN: FRANCE

MEANING:

OBABLY THE MOST WIDELY USED FRENCH SWEAR WORD, PUTAIN
AN SERVE YOU FOR A WIDE RANGE OF EMOTIONS! MEANING
'WHORE', THIS WORD IS COMMONLY USED IN PLACE OF 'FUCK'
IN ENGLISH, AND CAN BE USED TO EXPRESS ANGER, SADNESS,
JOY, AND ADMIRATION!

"¡ME CAGO EN DIOS!"

(ME-CA-GO-EN-DEE-OS)

LANGUAGE: SPANISH

ORIGIN: SPAIN

MEANING:

USED DURING TIMES OF ANNOYANCE AND SURPRISE, IN PLAC
OF THE ENGLISH 'FUCKING HELL!' OR 'DAMMIT', THIS SPANI
PHRASE TRANSLATES TO 'I SHIT ON GOD'.

"BURRO DE MERDA"

(BU-RU-DE-MEHR-DA)

LANGUAGE: PORTUGUESE

ORIGIN: PORTUGAL

MEANING:

PERFECT FOR WHEN YOU WANT TO CALL SOMEONE A 'DUMB SHIT', THIS PORTUGUESE INSULT TRANSLATES TO 'DONKEY OF SHIT', WHICH IS FAR BETTER THAN THE ENGLISH EQUIVALENT.

"DU BIST EIN ARSCHGEFICKTES SUPPENHUHN!"

(DU-BIST-EIN-ARSH-GE-FICK-TE-SOO-PEN-HOO

LANGUAGE: GERMAN

ORIGIN: GERMANY

MEANING:

Meaning 'you are a chicken that got fucked in the ass!', this German insult is a double whammy - there's no coming back from that one!

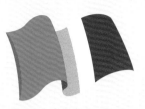

"TUA MAMMA BOCCHINARA"

(TU-A-MAMA-BOCK-I-NARA)

LANGUAGE: ITALIAN

ORIGIN: ITALY

MEANING:

THIS ITALIAN INSULT DIRECTLY MEANS 'YOUR MOM'S A
FLUFFER', A 'FLUFFER' BEING SOMEONE WHO KEEPS MALE
PORNSTARS AROUSED ON SET. HOWEVER, THIS IS COMMONLY
USED IN PLACE OF "SON OF A BITCH!"

"NA MOU KLASEIS TA'RXIDIA"

Θα μου κλάσεις τα αρχίδια

(NA-MOO-KLA-SIS-TA-HE-DIA)

LANGUAGE: GREEK

ORIGIN: GREECE

MEANING:

PERFECT FOR ANY TIME YOU WISH TO TELL SOMEONE TO QUIT
LITERALLY 'FART ON YOUR BALLS', THIS GREEK INSULT IS
USED TO CALL SOMEONE POWERLESS - GREAT FOR TAUNTING
SOMEONE IN A FIGHT!

"FITTHORA"

(FIT-HOAR-A)

LANGUAGE: SWEDISH

ORIGIN: SWEDEN

MEANING:

RANSLATING DIRECTLY AS 'CUNT WHORE', THIS PRETTY BRUTAL INSULT IS SURPRISINGLY COMMON IN SWEDEN. IT'S SAFE TO SAY THAT IT WILL NOT BE USED FOR ANY FUTURE IKEA FURNITURE NAMES.

"SATANS FORBANNA HÆSTKUK"

(SAH-TANS-FOUR-BAH-NA-HASTE-COOK)

LANGUAGE: NORWEGIAN

ORIGIN: NORWAY

MEANING:

THIS NORWEGIAN PROFANITY OPENS STRONG WITH 'SATAN'.
THE PHRASE THEN FINISHES AS 'SATAN'S FUCKING HORSECOCK'.
THIS IS USED AS AN EXCLAMATION, BUT IT IS ARGUABLY
STRONG ENOUGH TO BE USED UNIVERSALLY TO PISS A
NORWEGIAN SPEAKER OFF.

"BRUNDTHRÓ"

Brundþró

(BRUND-THROW)

LANGUAGE: Icelandic

ORIGIN: ICELAND

MEANING:

The Icelanders came up with a creative insult, translating literally to 'cum receptacle', which feels disgusting enough to be highly offensive. Use this in place of calling someone a wanker!

"PRIC PWDIN"

(PRIC-PUDDIN)

LANGUAGE: WELSH

ORIGIN: WALES

MEANING:

THIS WELSH INSULT IS PHONETIC AND TRANSLATES TO
'PUDDING WILLY'. IT CAN BE USED TO DESCRIBE AN IDIOT OR
SOMEONE YOU DON'T LIKE!

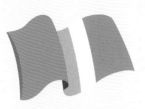

"GO MBEIRE AN DIABHAL THÚ"

(GOH-MERE-AN-DEE-A-WOOL-HOO)

LANGUAGE: IRISH

ORIGIN: IRELAND

MEANING:

THE IRISH ARE NOT KNOWN FOR MINCING THEIR WORDS, BUT THIS INSULT TRANSLATES AS 'MAY THE DEVIL CHOKE YOU' IN THE IRISH LANGUAGE, SO IT IS MORE OF A CREATIVE THAN OBSCENE PUT-DOWN!

"EŞŞOĞLUEŞŞEK"

(ESHO-LESHEK)

LANGUAGE: TURKISH

ORIGIN: TURKEY

MEANING:

TRANSLATING TO 'SON OF A DONKEY', THIS TURKISH INSULT IS ALSO COMMONLY USED IN PLACE OF 'SON OF A BITCH'. TH AMUSING THING ABOUT THIS INSULT IS THAT IT'S OFTEN USED BY FATHERS TO THEIR CHILDREN, WHILE INADVERTENTLY INSULTING THEMSELVES IN THE PROCESS!

"T'SHITOFT ZANA"

(TUH-SHE-TOFT-ZANNA)

LANGUAGE: ALBANIAN

ORIGIN: ALBANIA

MEANING:

WHILE IN ALBANIA THIS SWEAR WORD IS A FAIRLY COMMON PHRASE, WHEN TRANSLATED, IT ALMOST FEELS MEDIEVAL OR ENCHANTED. TRANSLATING TO 'MAY THE FAIRY BEWITCH YOU', THIS FUN CURSE WORD IS PERFECT FOR ALL AGES!

"KON DA TI GO NATRESE"

Кон да ти го натресе

(CON-DA-TEE-GO-NA-TREYS)

LANGUAGE: BULGARIAN

ORIGIN: BULGARIA

MEANING:

MEANING 'GO GET FUCKED BY A HORSE', THIS BULGARIAN INSULT IS CLASSIC, SIMPLE, AND TO THE POINT. SO IF YOU WANT TO TELL ANYONE TO PISS OFF, THIS CREATIVE PHRASE WILL HAVE LOCALS RUNNING FOR THE HILLS!

"DA TI JEBEM OCA"

(DAH TEE YEH-BEM OT-SAH)

LANGUAGE: MONTENEGRIN

ORIGIN: MONTENEGRO

MEANING:

...KING THE CLASSIC 'FUCK YOUR MOM' INSULT AND PUTTING A ...ALE SPIN ON IT, THIS MONTENEGRIN INSULT TAKES AIM AT ... MALE PARENT INSTEAD. TELLING THEM 'FUCK YOUR FATHER', ...MAKE SURE YOU DON'T USE THIS WHEN THEIR DAD IS NEARBY!

"AI GAAE DTAN HAA GLAP"

ไอ้แก่ตัณหากลับ

(AI-GAY-TAHN-HAA-GLAP)

LANGUAGE: THAI

ORIGIN: THAILAND

MEANING:

THIS MORE COMPLEX THAI INSULT TRANSLATES TO 'OLD MA
POSSESSED BY SEX DESPITE SENILITY', MAKING IT A TRIPLE
THREAT - OLD, SENILE, AND PERVERTED. OUCH.

"MÀY ĂN LÔNG DÁI CHẤM MUỐI"

(MAY-AN-LONG-DAY-CHAN-MOY)

LANGUAGE: VIETNAMESE

ORIGIN: VIETNAM

MEANING:

WITH THIS PHRASE, YOU CAN TELL PEOPLE 'YOU EAT PUBIC HAIR WITH A SALT DIP', WHICH SOUNDS LIKE IT SHOULD BE AN INSULT - UNLESS PUBIC HAIR AND SALT DIP IS A KILLER COMBO...

"TOFU NO KADO NI ATAMA WO UTTE SHINE"

豆腐の角に頭をぶつけて死ね

(TOFU-NO-KA-DOUGH-A-TAMMA-WO-EW-TEH-SHE-NE)

LANGUAGE: JAPANESE

ORIGIN: JAPAN

MEANING:

JAPAN IS ONE OF THE CULINARY EPICENTERS OF THE WORLD, SO IT'S NO SURPRISE THAT THIS INSULT INVOLVES FOOD. TRANSLATING TO 'GO HIT YOUR HEAD ON A BLOCK OF TOFU AND DIE', THIS ITERATION OF 'KILL YOURSELF' HAS A UNIQUE FINISH OVERALL.

"IDI U PIČKU MATERINU!"

(IDI-EW-PICH-KU-MAT-ER-INU)

LANGUAGE: CROATIAN

ORIGIN: CROATIA

MEANING:

'GO BACK INSIDE YOUR MOTHER'S PUSSY!' - GREAT TO USE WHEN YOU WANT TO TELL A CROATIAN TO FUCK OFF, BUT IN A WAY THAT JUST CUTS THAT LITTLE BIT DEEPER...

"ZKURVYSYN"

(SCURVY-SEEN)

LANGUAGE: CZECH

ORIGIN: CZECH REPUBLIC

MEANING:

Sometimes simple is best, and this popular Czech swear
is concise and to the point. Calling someone 'son of a
whore' is surely a great way to let your
grievances be known.

"MÅ DIN RØV KLTZØ, OG DINE ARME VÆRE FOR KORTE"

(MA-DIN-ROH-KLEW-OH-DEAN-AHM-E-VARE-FOR-COR-DUH)

LANGUAGE: DANISH

ORIGIN: DENMARK

MEANING:

More of a phrase said out of spite, in place of 'fuck you', this PG phrase is somehow more damning than any other NSFW word. Translating to 'may your ass itch and your arms be too short', this phrase is surprisingly hateful!

"JOU MA SE POES"

(YOW-MAH-SUH-POOS)

LANGUAGE: AFRIKAANS

ORIGIN: SOUTH AFRICA

MEANING:

TRANSLATING TO 'YOUR MOTHER'S CUNT', IT'S A DEROGATORY AFRIKAANS PHRASE THAT IS USED THROUGHOUT SOUTH AFRICA, WHICH CAN BE HIGHLY INSULTING TO A STRANGER, BUT ODDLY ENDEARING AMONG FRIENDS.

"CICI VUCHI"

(THI-THI-VOO-CHI)

LANGUAGE: FIJAN

ORIGIN: FIJI

MEANING:

HIS AMUSING SWEAR PHRASE TRANSLATES TO 'HAIRY ASSHOLE', WHICH COULD BE USED SIMPLY AS A DESCRIPTION OR AS AN INSULT. HOW WOULD YOU FEEL IF SOMEONE CALLED YOU A HAIRY ASSHOLE?

"VOI VITTUJEN KEVÄT"

(VOI-VIT-TOY-YEN-KAY-VAT)

LANGUAGE: FINNISH

ORIGIN: FINLAND

MEANING:

WHEN YOU FEEL LIKE ADDING SOME EXTRA **FLAIR** TO AN INSULT OR EXCLAMATION, THIS FINNISH EXPRESSION PROVIDES JUST THAT. TRANSLATING TO 'DAMN THE SPRINGTIME OF CUNTS', THIS EXPRESSIVE VARIATION OF THE STANDARD C WORD ADDS EXTRA SPICE TO YOUR LINGO!

"Q'LIS CH'UCH'Q'I"

ყლის ჭუჭყი

(KLIS-SHUSH-KEY)

LANGUAGE: GEORGIAN

ORIGIN: GEORGIA

MEANING:

If you want to call someone stupid in Georgia, this expression will certainly get the job done. However, please be aware that you would be calling someone 'PENIS SMEGMA' AS A DIRECT TRANSLATION!

"FEMEN DJOL KAKA SANTI W LA"

(FEM-ON-JOL-KAKA-S-ON-TEA-OU-LAH)

LANGUAGE: HAITIAN CREOLE

ORIGIN: HAITI

MEANING:

WHEN TELLING SOMEONE TO SIMPLY SHUT UP DOESN'T QUITE
CUT IT, THIS TRANSLATION WILL TELL THEM TO 'SHUT YOUR
STINKING, SHIT-FILLED MOUTH'... TOOTHBRUSH, ANYONE?

"AGYILAG ZOKNI"

(OG-EE-LAG-ZOCK-KNEE)

LANGUAGE:　HUNGARIAN

ORIGIN:　　　HUNGARY

MEANING:

Are you looking for a way to insult someone that feels fancy, but still brutal? This Hungarian insult translates to 'mentally (you are) a sock', essentially saying that there is absolutely nothing in your brain. Except maybe a sock.

"CUMI"

(CHEW-ME)

LANGUAGE: INDONESIAN

ORIGIN: INDONESIA

MEANING:

IN MANY CULTURES, CALLING PEOPLE ANIMALS CAN BE USED AS AN INSULT. TO OFFEND SOMEONE IN INDONESIA, YOU COULD CALL THEM 'CUMI', WHICH MEANS 'SQUID'.

"ZAHRE MĀR"

زهر مار

(ZAR-EY-MAR)

LANGUAGE: PERSIAN

ORIGIN: IRAN

MEANING:

THIS INSULT IS USED IN RESPONSE TO SOMEONE DURING AN ARGUMENT. YOU ARE SAYING THEY ARE TALKING 'SNAKE'S POISON', THE PERSIAN EQUIVALENT OF 'TALKING SHIT.

"SAMTI 'AL ZE KATZUTZ!"

!שמתי אל זה קצוץ

(SAM-TEE-AHL-ZUH-KAT-ZUH-TS)

LANGUAGE: HEBREW

ORIGIN: ISRAEL

MEANING:

IF YOU WANT TO TELL SOMEONE IN HEBREW THAT YOU SIMPL DON'T GIVE A FUCK, THIS SAYING FITS THE BILL. HOWEVER, THE DIRECT TRANSLATION IS 'I PUT MY CIRCUMCISED ONE O IT', WHICH IS AN INTERESTING WAY TO TELL SOMEONE YOU DON'T CARE.

"NYANI HAONI KUNDULE"

(KNEE-AH-KNEE-HOW-KNEE-KUN-DO-LAY)

LANGUAGE: SWAHILI

ORIGIN: KENYA

MEANING:

Perfect for saying to someone who is always quick to criticize, this phrase translates to 'a monkey doesn't see its own bottom'.

"NOEE UDONGSAL DEUL-EOSSNYA"

뇌에 우동사리 들었냐

(NOH-EE-EW-DONG-SALI-DAY-UL-ESS-KNEE-AH)

LANGUAGE: KOREAN

ORIGIN: SOUTH KOREA

MEANING:

NEXT TIME YOU WANT TO CALL SOMEONE STUPID, WHY NOT
SIMPLY ASK THEM IF THEY HAVE UDON NOODLES IN THEIR
HEAD INSTEAD OF A BRAIN? THAT WILL RATTLE
A FEW FEATHERS...

"GAK CHAK"

ກັກຄຸ

(GAHK-CHUCK)

LANGUAGE: LAO

ORIGIN: LAOS

MEANING:

HE PERFECT PUT DOWN IN ANY ARGUMENT—WHEN SOMEONE IS MAKING VERY VALID POINTS, INTERRUPT THEM AND SAY: 'YOUR BREATH SMELLS LIKE SHIT'. INSTANT ARGUMENT WINNER RIGHT THERE.

"EJ LASĪT SĒNES"

(EH-LASIT-SEH-NAS)

LANGUAGE: LATVIAN

ORIGIN: LATVIA

MEANING:

If someone is annoying you and you want them to leave you alone, this phrase will directly tell them to 'go pick mushrooms', which in Latvian, will get your point across perfectly.

"BANGSAT"

بڠسات

(BUHNG-SAHT)

LANGUAGE: MALAY

ORIGIN: MALAYSIA

MEANING:

Next time you want to call someone out for their sneaky behavior, this phrase will directly tell them they're a 'scoundrel' or 'bastard'. A perfect word to deter snack thieves!

"KUDAKUN"

ހުދަކުން

(KU-DA-KUN)

LANGUAGE: DHIVEHI

ORIGIN: MALDIVES

MEANING:

A MORE LIGHTHEARTED INSULT, THIS DHIVEHI WORD IS USED TO CALL SOMEONE WEAK OR A WIMP, BUT TRANSLATES TO 'SMALL FRY'. WE ARE LOVIN' IT!

"ILL, X'INHU/I LIBA!"

(IL-SHI-NOO-EE-LEE-BAH)

LANGUAGE: MALTESE

ORIGIN: MALTA

MEANING:

THE CHANCES ARE THAT YOU MAY WANT TO CALL SOMEONE A DICK, AND SHOULD YOU WISH TO DO IT IN MALTESE, THIS PHRASE IS PERFECT FOR USE. IT DIRECTLY TRANSLATES TO 'OH, WHAT A SPERM HE IS!', WHICH IS THE SAME THING, RIGHT?

"KÁG KO CHORÓ"

काग को छोरो

(KAHG-KOH CHO-ROH)

LANGUAGE: NEPALI

ORIGIN: NEPAL

MEANING:

IN NEPAL, IF SOMEONE CALLED YOU A 'SON OF A CROW', YOU MIGHT NOT BE OFFENDED. IT'S ACTUALLY A TERM OFTEN USED WHEN SOMEONE DOES SOMETHING MISCHIEVOUS AND CUNNING, BUT IT ALMOST FEELS LIKE A COMPLIMENT!

"KANKERHOND"

(CAN-KER-HOO-ND)

LANGUAGE: DUTCH

ORIGIN: THE NETHERLANDS

MEANING:

THROWING DOGS INTO INSULTS IS NOT SOMETHING NEW (JUST THINK OF THE CLASSIC 'BITCH'). HOWEVER, THE DUTCH JUST DO IT WITH MORE FINESSE. AND BY FINESSE, WE MEAN THEY STILL CALL YOU A DOG. NOT JUST ANY DOG THOUGH. A CANCER DOG.

"PŌKOKOHUA"

(POH-KOKO-HOO-AH)

LANGUAGE: MAORI

ORIGIN: NEW ZEALAND

MEANING:

THIS PHRASE IS THE MAORI WAY TO CALL SOMEONE A FUCKWIT.
HOWEVER, IT IS GENERALLY REGARDED AS A PRETTY EXTREME
INSULT AND TRANSLATES DIRECTLY TO 'BOILED HEAD'.

"SUPÓT"

(SOO-POT)

LANGUAGE: FILIPINO

ORIGIN: PHILIPPINES

MEANING:

In the Philippines, calling someone this phrase essentially means calling them uncircumcised, which ordinarily doesn't seem offensive. However, this word is actually used to demean or insult men!

"NIE BYŁEŚ JESZCZE W CZOŁGU

(NYEH BI-WEHSH YESH-CHEH V CHOH-WE-GOO)

LANGUAGE: POLISH

ORIGIN: POLAND

MEANING:

The phrase 'Nie byłeś jeszcze w czołgu?' translates to 'Have you ever been in a tank?' It's a humorous way o implying that someone is inexperienced or clueless. Cute.

"USCAMIAS CHILOTII PE CRUCEA MATII"

(OOS-KA-MY-ASS KEE-LOH-TEE PEH KROO-CHEA MAHT-EE)

LANGUAGE: ROMANIAN

ORIGIN: ROMANIA

MEANING:

Directly translating to 'I shit on your mother's cross!' this insult carries a degree of theatrics and involves a maternal insult, which seems to be a universal theme!

"KURVA"

Курва

(KOOR-VAH)

LANGUAGE: SERBIAN

ORIGIN: SERBIA

MEANING:

IT'S A HIGHLY OFFENSIVE TERM IN SERBIAN. IT LITERALLY MEANS 'WHORE' OR 'PROSTITUTE' AND IS OFTEN USED AS A GENERAL INSULT TOWARDS SOMEONE, IMPLYING THAT THEY HAVE A PROMISCUOUS BACKGROUND.

MELO MELO LOU PI"

(MEH-LOH-MEH-LOH-LOO-PEE)

LANGUAGE: SAMOAN

ORIGIN: SAMOA

MEANING:

IS LOOSELY TRANSLATES TO 'YOUR VAGINA IS GLITTERY', AND
T'S AN INSULT IN SAMOAN. HOWEVER, IT'S HARD TO THINK
OF HOW A GLITTERY VAGINA WOULD BE A BAD THING...

"JE TO POPIČI"

(YE-TOE-POH-PEE-CHEE)

LANGUAGE: SLOVAK

ORIGIN: SLOVAKIA

MEANING:

THESE RUDE WORDS ARE USED TO EXPRESS FRUSTRATION OR ANNOYANCE, ALTHOUGH IT CAN OFTEN BE SAID IN JEST. HOWEVER, IT DIRECTLY TRANSLATES AS 'IT'S A LITTLE BITCH' WHICH SAYS IT ALL ABOUT THE PERSON YOU'RE INSULTING.

"AYEEYODA AY CUN FATADAY"

(AYE-EE-YOH-DA-AI-CUN-FAT-AH-DAY)

LANGUAGE: SOMALI

ORIGIN: SOMALIA

MEANING:

WHEN GOING FOR SOMEONE'S MOTHER JUST ISN'T ENOUGH, WHY NOT GO FOR THEIR GRANDMOTHER? THIS INSULT, TRANSLATING TO 'YOUR GRANDMOTHER EATS MY ASS,' IS SURE TO RUFFLE SOME FEATHERS.

"HARNA LIALKA, TA TUPA"

гарна лялька, та тупа

(HAHR-NAH-LEE-AHL-KAH-TAH-TOO-PAH)

LANGUAGE: UKRAINIAN

ORIGIN: UKRAINE

MEANING:

THIS IS AN INSULT THAT ACTUALLY IS MORE OF A BACKHANDE COMPLIMENT. ROUGHLY MEANING 'PRETTY DOLL, BUT DUMB IT IS USED WHEN SOMEONE IS VERY PRETTY, BUT ALSO PRETTY STUPID.

"TEEZAK HAMRA"

طيزك حمرا

(TEE-ZACK-HAM-RA)

LANGUAGE: ARABIC

ORIGIN: UNITED ARAB EMIRATES

MEANING:

LITERALLY MEANING 'YOUR ASS IS RED', THIS INSULT IS
USUALLY USED IN PLACE OF CALLING SOMEONE A DUMBASS.

"KRISNERA ZHAZH TAN VRED"

(CRISH-NEH-RA -ZHAZH-TAN-VRED)

LANGUAGE: ARMENIAN

ORIGIN: ARMENIA

MEANING:

THIS QUIPPY OBSCENITY COMBINES A SEXUAL VIOLATION AND VERMIN; TWO THINGS THAT MAKE A GREAT INSULT. TRANSLATING TO 'LET THE RATS EJACULATE ON YOU', THIS UNUSUAL INSULT CAN BE USED IN PLACE OF THE CLASSIC 'FUCK YOU!'

"PEHN DI SIRI"

پہن دی سری

(PE-HUN-DEE-SIRI)

LANGUAGE: URDU

ORIGIN: PAKISTAN

MEANING:

LESS COMMONLY USED NOW, THERE ARE STILL AREAS OF PAKISTAN THAT RECOGNIZE URDU INSULTS, SUCH AS THIS ONE WHICH MEANS 'CURSE ON YOUR SISTER'S HEAD'.

"CHUDMU TOR PASAI SNEHA"

চুদমু ত০োর পাশাই স্নহে

(CHUD-MOO-TOR-PASH-ES-NEY-HA)

LANGUAGE: BENGALI

ORIGIN: BANGLADESH

MEANING:

TRANSLATING TO 'PROSTITUTE WHO DOES ANAL', THIS BENGALI
SWEAR SUCCEEDS IN PROVIDING A LITTLE MORE DETAIL ON THE
KIND OF PROSTITUTE YOU ARE CALLING THEM.

"KAB TY NA SVET PRAZ DUPU GLIADZEU"

Каб ты на свет праз дупу глядзеў

(CAB-TE-NA-SVET-PRAZ-DOO-POO-GLYAD-ZYO)

LANGUAGE: BELARUSIAN

ORIGIN: BELARUS

MEANING:

THIS BELARUSIAN INSULT IS A MORE CREATIVE PHRASE WHEN TRANSLATED, MEANING 'I WISH YOU WOULD SEE THE WORLD THROUGH YOUR ASS'. COMPLEX AND INSULTING, WITHOUT RINGING SOMEONE'S MOTHER INTO IT - GOOD JOB BELARUS!

"LLE HOLMA VE' EDAN"

(LEH-HOL-MAH-VEH-EE-DAN)

LANGUAGE: ELVISH

ORIGIN: MIDDLE EARTH

MEANING:

Translating to 'you smell like a human', this Elvish insult won't get you very far on Planet Earth, given that everyone smells human. However, in Middle Earth this insult is sure to piss off an elf or two!

"TOLGUS"

(TOLL-GUSS)

LANGUAGE: ESTONIAN

ORIGIN: ESTONIA

MEANING:

ROUGHLY TRANSLATING TO 'THE ONE WHO DANGLES ALONG IN LIFE', THIS PLAYFUL AND PG-13 INSULT IS PERFECT FOR CALLING SOMEONE USELESS.

"BILO-HEAD"

(BEE-LOW-HEAD)

LANGUAGE: FIJAN

ORIGIN: FIJI

MEANING:

THIS PLAYFUL INSULT TRANSLATES TO 'COCONUT HEAD' AND IS MEANT TO BE USED WHEN SOMEONE IS BEING STUPID OR ABSENT-MINDED. IT'S ALSO VERY FUN TO SAY AND IS UNLIKELY TO OFFEND ANYONE TOO DEEPLY!

"ULLU KA PATTA"

उल्लू का पट्ठा

(ULLU-KA-PAT-TA)

LANGUAGE: HINDI

ORIGIN: INDIA

MEANING:

TRANSLATING TO 'SON OF AN OWL', THIS NICHE INSULT IS USED COMMONLY IN CULTURES WHERE OWLS ARE CONSIDERED LAZY AND STUPID. OUCH

"EZ DILÊ TE DIXWIM

ئەز دڵێ تە دیخۆنێم

(EZ DEE-LEH TEH DEE-KHWIM)

LANGUAGE: KURDISH

ORIGIN: IRAQ

MEANING:

THIS PHRASE MIGHT NOT SEEM THAT BAD, AS IT TRANSLATES T
'I EAT YOUR HEART,' BUT IT'S MEANT TO EXPRESS DISDAIN O
ANGER TOWARDS SOMEONE AND CAN BE SEEN
AS HIGHLY OFFENSIVE.

"MAKALDAM"

макалдам

(MAH-KAHL-DAHM)

LANGUAGE: KYRGYZ

ORIGIN: KYRGYZSTAN

MEANING:

THIS LIGHT-HEARTED PHRASE IS NOT SO MUCH AN INSULT, BUT IS A FUNNY WAY TO CALL SOMEONE 'SCATTERBRAINED' OR 'AIRHEAD', IMPLYING THAT SOMEONE IS A BIT ABSENT-MINDED OR NOT VERY SERIOUS.

"MOCHOCHO"

(MOH-KOH-CHOH)

LANGUAGE: SOTHO

ORIGIN: LESOTHO

MEANING:

IF THERE IS ONE RULE WHEN ATTEMPTING TO SPEAK SOTHO, IT IS TO NOT INSULT SOMEONE'S PARTNER. UNLESS YOU WANT TO CAUSE SOME SERIOUS ISSUES FOR YOURSELF, IN WHICH CASE THIS PHRASE, TRANSLATING TO 'PROSTITUTE', SHOULD DO THE TRICK.

"CHUPA MEU PAU"

(SHOO-PAH MEH-OO POW)

LANGUAGE: BRAZILIAN PORTUGUESE

ORIGIN: BRAZIL

MEANING:

THIS INSULT HAILS FROM PORTUGUESE SPEAKERS IN BRAZIL AND IS PERFECT TO USE WHEN SOMEONE HAS REALLY GOT ON UR LAST NERVE. THIS INSULT DIRECTLY TRANSLATES TO 'SUCK MY POLE' AND I'M SURE YOU CAN WORK OUT WHICH 'POLE' THEY'RE REFERRING TO...

"¡CHINGA TU MADRE!"

(CHIN-GA-TOO-MAH-DRE)

LANGUAGE: SPANISH

ORIGIN: MEXICO

MEANING:

THIS SIMPLE SPANISH PHRASE IS FAR MORE COMMON IN MEXICO AND SOUTH AMERICA, AND TRANSLATES BEAUTIFUL AND SIMPLY TO 'FUCK YOUR MOTHER!' SO USE THIS AT YOU OWN DISCRETION!

"DANK FARRIK"

(DANK FAH-RIK)

LANGUAGE: MANDO'A

ORIGIN: MANDALORE

MEANING:

IF YOU EVER FIND YOURSELF CROSSING INTER-GALACTIC PATHS WITH AN ANGRY MANDALORIAN, YOU MIGHT HEAR THEM EXPRESS 'DANK FARRIK!' IT IS USED IN PLACE OF 'DAMN!' OR 'FUCK!', BUT ITS DIRECT TRANSLATION REMAINS UNKNOWN. MAYBE YOU COULD ASK THEM FOR US?

"KOTU KELIYA"

කො ටු කැලෙ 'යා

(KO-TWO-KELL-EE-YAH)

LANGUAGE: SINHALA

ORIGIN: SRI LANKA

MEANING:

TRANSLATING TO 'MONKEY TAIL', THIS IS A GREAT SAFE-FOR
WORK TERM FOR SOMEONE WHO IS MISCHIEVOUS AND CHEEK

"PODA PUNDAI"

படோட பூண்டை

(POH-DAH-PUUN-DAI)

LANGUAGE: TAMIL

ORIGIN: SINGAPORE

MEANING:

IF YOU REALLY WANT SOMEONE TO LEAVE YOU ALONE, THIS PHRASE ESSENTIALLY TELLS THEM TO 'GO AWAY, CUNT!'. THE ADDITION OF THE 'C' WORD ADDS AN EXTRA STING...

"KHAR KHÜÜR"

Хар хүүр

(CH-A-R CH-EE-R)

LANGUAGE: MONGOLIAN

ORIGIN: MONGOLIA

MEANING:

IN MONGOLIAN, KHAR KHÜÜR TRANSLATES TO 'BLACK CORPSE
IT'S A RATHER BLUNT INSULT, SUGGESTING THAT SOMEONE
IS ABOUT AS LIVELY AND USEFUL AS A ROCK. IT'S THE KIND O
PHRASE YOU MIGHT EXPECT FROM AN OLD GRIZZLED COWBOY!

"FAI HOOSI"

(FAY-WHO-SEE)

LANGUAGE: TONGAN

ORIGIN: TONGA

MEANING:

THIS UNIQUE INSULT IS TO THE POINT, CALLING THE UNLUCKY RECIPIENT A 'HORSE FUCKER'. PRETTY SHARP AND SURE TO PUT ANY TONGAN SPEAKER IN THEIR PLACE.

"QI-YAH!"

(KEY-YAH)

LANGUAGE: KLINGON

ORIGIN: STAR TREK

MEANING:

This swear is so offensive to native Klingon speakers that it has no direct translation into English! Roughly translating as '*?!#@', this should only be used in very extreme circumstances when you really want to offend a member of the alien race!

"QAVALLUQ"

каваллуӄ

(KAH-VAH-LOOK)

LANGUAGE: YUPIK

ORIGIN: NORTHEASTERN RUSSIA

MEANING:

Perfect if you encounter an Inuit from the Yupik region of northeastern Russia and some parts of laska, this simple insult is to be used when someone is eing annoying, and you want to call them an asshole. Simple yet effective.

"MATER TUA CALIGAS GERIT"

(MATTER-TOO-A-CA-LEE-GAS-JE-RIT)

LANGUAGE: LATIN

ORIGIN: VATICAN CITY

MEANING:

UNFORTUNATELY, EVEN BACK IN ANCIENT TIMES WHEN LATIN WAS WIDELY SPOKEN, MOTHERS WERE NOT SAFE. THIS TRANSLATES TO 'YOUR MOTHER WEARS LEGIONARY BOOTS' AN COULD PERHAPS BE THE OLDEST 'YOUR MOTHER' JOKE IN EXISTENCE.

"AFAITAPAGESOS"

(A-FAT-A-PA-SHEZ-OS)

LANGUAGE: CATALAN

ORIGIN: ANDORRA

MEANING:

IN CATALAN, IF YOU FIND YOURSELF IN A POSITION WHERE YOU NEED TO ACCUSE SOMEONE OF BEING A SCAMMER, THIS INSULT DOES JUST THAT... BY CALLING THEM A 'FARMER SHAVER'.

"SELINOKH"

(SEH-LEE-NOKH)

LANGUAGE: SYRIAC

ORIGIN: SYRIA

MEANING:

If you want to offend someone in the Assyrian region, this word will simply say 'fuck you!' A classic of our time, this surely is a staple that can't be forgotten!

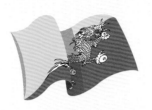

"JIK RI DOJE"

འཇིག་རི་རྡོ་རྗེ།

(JIK-REE-DOH-JAY)

LANGUAGE: DZONGKHA

ORIGIN: BHUTAN

MEANING:
THIS SIMPLE PHRASE IN BHUTAN MIGHT SEEM INNOCENT, BUT ACTUALLY STANDS FOR 'ASSHOLE'. IT'S PRETTY SATISFYING TO SAY TOO!

"SWERA NYOKO"

(SWER-A-NYO-KO)

LANGUAGE: KIRUNDI

ORIGIN: BURUNDI

MEANING:

Sometimes, when insulting someone, the classics are classics for a reason. This is the Kirundi phrase for 'fuck your mother', which is definitely to the point.

"A KHVAK"

អាខ្វាក់

(AH K-VAK)

LANGUAGE: KHMER

ORIGIN: CAMBODIA

MEANING:

THE CLASSIC 'KHVAK' MOMENT. IT'S THE KHMER WAY OF ~~S~~YING 'BLESS THEIR HEART, BUT THEY'RE ABOUT AS CLUELESS AS ~~A~~ CAT IN A ROOM FULL OF ROCKING CHAIRS'. SO, NEXT TIME ~~S~~OMEONE ASKS IF THEY CAN MICROWAVE THEIR PHONE, JUST USE THIS SIMPLE PHRASE!

"SEE YOR FRY PAN YANSH"

(SEE-YOUR-FRY-PAN-NYAN-SH)

LANGUAGE: NIGERIAN PIDGIN

ORIGIN: NIGERIAN

MEANING:

Nigerian Pidgin is an English-based Creole language and some phrases can be understood through their use of English words. Take this phrase, translated to 'look at you, flat ass', which compares their ass to a frying pan!

"PAADAR GANDICHYA"

पाडार गंदीच्या

(PAA-DAR-GUN-DI-CHI-YA)

LANGUAGE: MARATHI

ORIGIN: INDIA

MEANING:

THIS SLIGHTLY MORE INNOCENT INSULT HAILS FROM THE MUMBAI REGION OF INDIA AND SIMPLY TRANSLATES TO 'FARTY ASSED' - AND WE ALL KNOW SOMEONE WHO DESERVES TO BE CALLED THAT!

"SILBABOT"

(SIL-BA-BO)

LANGUAGE: AMHARIC

ORIGIN: ETHIOPIA

MEANING:

EVEN IN ETHIOPIA, YOU MIGHT WANT TO SAY THAT SOMEON
IS BEING A NUISANCE! THIS DIRECTLY TRANSLATES TO 'YOU
ARE THE FATTY LAYER ON WARM MILK', WHICH IS CERTAINLY
SPECIFIC INSULT!

"DUPOT ḰE TI GO RASCEPAM"

дупот ḱе ти го расцепам

(DUH-POHT KYAY TEE GOH RAHS-TSE-PAHM)

LANGUAGE: MACEDONIAN

ORIGIN: NORTH MACEDONIA

MEANING:

IDEAL FOR AN AGGRESSIVE SITUATION WHEN YOU WANT TO TELL SOMEONE THAT YOU WILL 'FUCK THEM UP'. EXCEPT WHAT YOU'RE ACTUALLY SAYING IS 'I WILL TEAR YOUR ASS APART'. SLIGHTLY MORE INTENSE, BUT ALSO MORE THREATENING.

"CEMENTERIO TIMBRE"

(CEMENT-EH-RIO-TIM-BRE)

LANGUAGE: GUARANÍ

ORIGIN: PARAGUAY

MEANING:

GUARANÍ IS SIMILAR TO SPANISH; HOWEVER, IT HAS SLIGHTLY DIFFERENT PHRASES AND COLLOQUIAL INSULTS. TAKE THIS PHRASE, FOR INSTANCE, WHICH WOULD BE CALLING SOMEONE A 'CEMETERY BELL'. IN PARAGUAY, IT WOULD BE ACCUSING SOMEONE OF BEING DEADBEAT AND USELESS.

"EWURE OSHI"

(EE-WUR-E-OSHI)

LANGUAGE: YORUBA

ORIGIN: NIGERIA

MEANING:

Another animal-based insult, this Yoruba phrase anslates to 'stupid goat', which is pretty damn funny.

''DUMPADENCHUTAA

డుంపదొంచుతా

(DUM-PA-DEN-CHEW-TA)

LANGUAGE: Telugu

ORIGIN: INDIA

MEANING:

Loosely translating to 'I'll cut your dick off', this
Telugu insult could be seen more as a catastrophic
threat... Here's hoping they're just all talk...

"MUKHA KANG TAE"

(MUK-HA-KONG-TAI)

LANGUAGE: TAGALOG

ORIGIN: PHILIPPINES

MEANING:

SOMETIMES, SIMPLY TELLING SOMEONE THEY LOOK LIKE SHIT IS THE PERFECT INSULT. TO THE POINT, AND YOU HAVE A 60% CHANCE OF MAKING THEM CRY, SO THIS TAGALOG INSULT REALLY HITS THE MARK.

"THERI MA DE LUN NAAL GOBI JAMDI"

(TARE-E-MAR-DEE-LUND-NAL-GO-BEE-JAM-DEE)

LANGUAGE: PUNJABI

ORIGIN: PAKISTAN

MEANING:

OK, THIS ONE IS ROUGH – BUT ALSO, QUITE CREATIVE!
TRANSLATING TO 'CAULIFLOWER GROWS IN YOUR MOM'S
DICK', THIS GROSS INSULT IS SURE TO TAKE ANYONE'S
BREATH AWAY!

"WA NDAYA WE!"

(WAH-UHN-DAY-A-WEH!)

LANGUAGE: KINYARWANDA

ORIGIN: RWANDA

MEANING:

ANOTHER CLASSIC, IF SOMEONE ANGERS YOU IN RWANDA, JUST SAY THIS, WHICH TRANSLATES TO 'YOU BITCH!' A TRULY WELL EXECUTED OG INSULT.

"GAM YU LOU"

金魚佬

(GAM-YOU-LOO)

LANGUAGE: CANTONESE

ORIGIN: CHINA

MEANING:

MEANING 'GOLDFISH MAN', THIS ESSENTIALLY CALLS SOMEONE A PEDOPHILE, SUGGESTING THAT THEY LURE SMALL CHILDREN TO THEM WITH BAGS OF PET GOLDFISH. CONSIDER IT AN EASTERN ITERATION OF SOMEONE WHO DRIVES A WHITE VAN WITH 'FREE CANDY' ON THE SIDE!

"DAN BANZA"

(DAN-BAN-ZA)

LANGUAGE: HAUSA

ORIGIN: NIGERIA

MEANING:

Keeping it simple, in Hausa, this swear just means 'bastard'. Sometimes the more classic swears are the most effective!

"GAY KOCKEN OFFEN YOM!"

סי וﬠﬦﬞﬞוﬞﬞ וﬦﬞﬞﬞﬞﬞאﬞﬞﬞﬞ ﬞﬞﬞﬞﬞﬞﬞ

(GAY-KACHEN-AFEN-YAHM)

LANGUAGE: YIDDISH

ORIGIN: ISRAEL

MEANING:

ROUGHLY TRANSLATING TO 'GO SHIT IN THE OCEAN', THIS
YIDDISH PHRASE SHOULD BE USED WHEN YOU WANT TO TELL
SOMEONE TO GO AWAY BUT WITH A LITTLE MORE FLAIR!

"ASU RAIMU"

(ASS-EW-RAI-MOO)

LANGUAGE: JAVANESE

ORIGIN: INDONESIA

MEANING:

THE PERFECT WAY TO INSULT SOMEONE. NOT NECESSARILY A PROFANITY, BUT PRETTY WOUNDING - CALLING THEM A 'DOG FACE'. THAT'S GOT TO HURT.

"DHEELA LUND NI OLAAD"

ઢીલા લુંડ ની ઓલાદ

(DEE-LA-LUND-KNEE-OH-LAD)

LANGUAGE: GUJARATI

ORIGIN: INDIA

MEANING:

A NICELY CREATIVE CURSE WORD (WELL... PHRASE, REALLY), THIS
TRANSLATES TO 'PRODUCT OF A LOOSE PENIS'. NICE THAT THE
MEN ARE GETTING SOME INSULTS ABOUT THEM TOO - IT'S
ALL ABOUT BALANCE.

"LIKATA"

(LI-CAT-AH)

LANGUAGE: LINGALA

ORIGIN: THE DRC

MEANING:

THIS SIMPLE AND PUNCHY WORD IS A PERFECT CURSE FOR ANY SITUATION. MEANING 'COCK', THIS COULD BE A NAME, AN EXPRESSION OF ANGER, OR JUST TO DESCRIBE YOUR... WELL, YEAH!

"PERHOT' PODZALUPNAYA"

Перхоть подзалупная

(PIER-HOT-POD-ZA-LUP-NAYA)

LANGUAGE: RUSSIAN

ORIGIN: RUSSIA

MEANING:

Calling someone 'Peehole dandruff' probably wouldn'
be your go-to insult. But in Russia, this confusing,
gross and funny insult is popular – just don't say it
to Putin though...

KHANGE KHODAH"

خنگ خ ادا

(KAN-GEH-KO-DA)

LANGUAGE: FARSI

ORIGIN: IRAN

MEANING:
TRANSLATING TO 'SCREW UP OF GOD', THIS SEEMINGLY PC
INSULT IS SURE TO BRING ANY LOCAL TO TEARS.

"PLUM, DWAM, AND BRICH"

(PLUM, DW-AHM, B-RICH)

LANGUAGE: SIMLISH

ORIGIN: SIMNATION

MEANING:

NOT ONE, NOT TWO, BUT THREE CUSS WORDS THAT ARE POPULAR AMONGST THE SIM POPULATION AND CAN OFTEN BE SEEN WHEN CURSING! THEIR DIRECT MEANINGS ARE UNKNOWN, BUT THESE SHOULD BE USED WHEN EXCLAIMING, IN PLACE OF WORDS LIKE 'SHIT, DAMN, FUCK'. YOU GET THE PICTURE!